The Warrior Mom's Guide to Loving Unexpectedly

Guardianship, Fostering & Adoption with Faith and Fierce Love

Shaundra M. G. Harris

The Warrior Mom's Guide to Loving Unexpectedly

Guardianship, Fostering & Adoption with Faith and Fierce Love

Author: Shaundra M. G. Harris
Publisher: Shaun The Mom Publishing

© 2025 Shaundra M. G. Harris
All rights reserved.

Paperback ISBN: 978-1-969446-09-2
Hardback ISBN: 978-1-969446-19-1

First Edition

No part of this publication may be reproduced, stored in a retrieval system, or transmitted in any form without written permission from the author, except by reviewers or educators using brief quotations with proper citation.

Publisher: Shaun The Mom Publishing
Printed in the United States

www.warriormomacademy.com

Disclaimer
This book is intended for informational and inspirational purposes only. The content reflects the personal experiences, opinions, and insights of the author and should not be considered a substitute for professional medical, legal, financial, educational, therapeutic, or spiritual advice.

While the author shares tools, tips, and resources that have been personally helpful, every situation is unique. Readers are encouraged to consult with qualified professionals before making decisions regarding health, finances, homeschooling, parenting, estate planning, or other matters discussed in this book.

Some links or references may be affiliate links, meaning the author may receive a small commission at no extra cost to you if you choose to purchase through those links. These recommendations are made in good faith and reflect resources the author personally uses or believes may be helpful.

Any printable templates, checklists, or workbook materials included are for personal use only and may not be distributed, sold, or used commercially without written permission from the author.

The author and publisher expressly disclaim any liability arising directly or indirectly from the use or misuse of any information, tools, or resources included in this book

To every woman who answered the call—even when her hands were full, her heart was breaking, and her strength felt spent.

To the sisters, aunties, godmothers, and kin who stepped up, stepped in, and stayed.

To my son—my heart in human form.
To my sister—your love made me a mother again.

This is for you.

A Note to the Reader: You're Not Alone

If you feel invisible, overwhelmed, or underqualified—take heart.

You are seen.
You are chosen.
You are not failing—you are fiercely loving in the middle of complicated circumstances.

Let this book be a safe place to land, a place to remember that love doesn't always look like biology or a picture-perfect beginning.

Sometimes love looks like court papers and case plans.
Sometimes love looks like midnight prayers over a child who didn't come from your womb—but was always meant for your heart.

This is the warrior mom guide to loving unexpectedly.

Let's begin.

Table of Contents

Introduction... 2

    Hey Mama,..2

    How to Use This Book...5

    When Life Doesn't Ask, It Demands 7

    From Call to Courtroom 9

    My Story: Guardian, Foster Mother, and Adoptive Parent 12

    Why I'm Telling You This 16

Part I: The Unexpected Call.......................... 18

    Chapter 1: The Day Everything Changed — Becoming a Medical Guardian......................... 18

    Chapter 2: What Happens When a Child Tests Positive at Birth... 22

    Chapter 3: Emergency Guardianship — What You Need to Know.. 25

    Chapter 4: Love and Legalities — Why I Became a Foster Parent..................................... 28

    Side Quest: Emergency Planning Toolkit for Warrior Moms 31

Part II: Navigating Foster Care as Family. 37

    Chapter 5: The First Night Home — Baby, Equipment & Overwhelm 38

    Chapter 6: Becoming a Licensed Foster Parent (Fast!)... 41

Chapter 7: Loving Through the System — Home Visits, Court, and Red Tape 44

Chapter 8: Supporting the Birth Parent Without Losing Yourself 47

Part III: Adoption and the Power of Yes 50

Chapter 9: When Parental Rights Are Terminated 51

Chapter 10: Saying Yes in the Courtroom (and What That Means) 54

Chapter 11: Oakland County Adoption Day — Our New Beginning 57

Chapter 12: Helping a Medically Fragile Child Thrive 60

Part IV: Family, Grief & False Narratives . 63

Chapter 13: The Rumors Hurt, But I Know My Truth 64

Chapter 14: Loving My Sister While Telling the Truth 67

Chapter 15: The Grief No One Prepared Me For 70

Chapter 16: When Family Feels Divided — Speaking Up With Grace 72

Part V: Planning for the Unplanned 75

Chapter 17: How to Legally Name a Guardian for Your Child 76

Chapter 18: How to Become a Foster Parent in Your State 79

Chapter 19: Kinship & Family Adoption —
What You Need to Know 82

Chapter 20: Getting Your House, Heart &
Finances Ready for a Child 85

Part VI: The Legacy of Preparation 88

Chapter 21: Why Every Parent Needs a
Guardian Plan 89

Chapter 22: Leaving Instructions — Wills,
Letters & Life Insurance 92

Chapter 22 (Part 2): Legacy Planning – My
Instructions of Love 95

Chapter 23: Creating a Legacy of Love (and
Legal Readiness) 97

Chapter 24: Helping Other Moms Do the Same
.... 100

Letter from the Author 102

Scriptures for Love, Courage & Trust 103

Book Club / Group Discussion Questions . 104

Glossary of Key Terms 106

Resources & Recommended Reading 111

The Warrior Mom's Guide™ Book Series . 115

About the Author 118

Introduction

Hey Mama,

If you've ever been thrust into motherhood by tragedy, by duty, or by surprise—you're not alone.

Whether you're raising your own babies, your sister's babies, or someone else's entirely, you've likely had to make impossible choices with very little help.

This book was born from one of the hardest seasons of my life. But it's not just a story about hardship—it's about hope, healing, and how we rise.

It's a guide for planning what most people never want to think about: guardianship, fostering, adoption, and what happens to our children when life flips the script.

I didn't have a plan when that phone call came. I had to figure it out the hard way. My prayer is that this book gives you tools, courage, and clarity—so your children, nieces, nephews, and god babies don't fall through the cracks when life gets messy.

When Love Finds You Unexpectedly

I didn't plan to become a second mom.
I didn't fill out an application. I didn't attend a parenting class.

What I did was say yes in the middle of a storm.
My nephew needed someone.
My sister was fighting a medical battle that left her unable to care for him. And when the phone rang, I wasn't ready—but I knew I couldn't say no.

This is how unexpected motherhood often begins—not with a baby shower or birth plan, but with a court date, a diagnosis, or a desperate call in the night.

Whether you're caring for a relative's child, fostering a child from the system, or stepping into the sacred journey of adoption, you're not just "filling in."
You are parenting with purpose.

This Book Is for the Mom Who…

- Stepped in out of love, not legal obligation.
- Is learning how to parent a child who's been through trauma.
- Is navigating case workers, court hearings, or confusing family dynamics.
- Wonders if she's "really" a mom, even though her heart knows the answer.

- Needs help sorting out the emotions, logistics, and spiritual weight of it all.
- Wants to raise this child with love, structure, stability, and faith.

Whether your guardianship was temporary or permanent...
Whether your adoption is open or closed...
Whether you're still waiting for the system to make decisions...
This book was written to help you love unexpectedly—with fierce commitment and holy grace.

How to Use This Book

Read it as a devotional.
Use it as a workbook.
Cry when you need to. Highlight the pages that hit deep.
Bring it to court appointments or quiet time with God.

Inside, you'll find:
- Real stories from my own guardianship and adoption journey
- Practical tools to help you understand legal terms, systems, and processes
- Devotional guidance to care for your spiritual and emotional health
- Reflection spaces to process grief, hope, frustration, and joy

At the end of every chapter, you'll see a RAPA section (Reflection • Affirmation • Prayer • Action).

Reflection – Journal your thoughts and emotions

Affirmation – Speak truth over your role and your child's future

Prayer – Invite God into the moment

Action – Take one small step forward

🐝 Reflection | Prayer | Affirmation | Action

Introduction

Reflection

Think about a time when life surprised you with a responsibility you didn't expect. How did you respond—with fear, hesitation, courage, or faith? Write down what rose up in you.

Affirmation

"I am chosen for this moment. God equips me for every role He calls me into."

Prayer

Lord, thank You for calling me, even when I feel unprepared. Help me see unexpected assignments not as burdens, but as opportunities to love deeply. Give me wisdom, patience, and courage for the children You've entrusted to me. Amen.

Action Step

Write a short note to yourself: Why am I reading this book right now? Keep it in the front cover as a reminder when things get hard.

When Life Doesn't Ask, It Demands

I didn't wake up and decide to become a foster parent.
I didn't dream of becoming a guardian while my sister lay in a hospital bed in a coma.
And I certainly didn't plan to adopt a newborn in crisis.
But I did.
I answered a call—literally and spiritually—and everything in my life changed.

This book is about that call. It's about what happens when you go from auntie to mama overnight, when legal systems collide with love, and when you're forced to navigate family, grief, and paperwork all at once.

It's not easy. And it's not always pretty. But it's necessary.

Here, you'll find real talk, legal tips, planning steps, and reflections for every woman who finds herself raising a child she didn't birth—but who was always meant to be hers.
Your kids deserve a plan. Your family deserves peace. And you, Mama, deserve to be ready.

Let's get into it.

🕊 Reflection | Prayer | Affirmation | Action

When Life Doesn't Ask

Reflection

Have you ever faced a responsibility you didn't choose? How did it shape you? How did God meet you in that moment?

Affirmation

"I may not have chosen this path, but God has chosen me for it."

Prayer

Father, when life places demands on me that I don't feel ready for, remind me that Your strength is made perfect in my weakness. Help me trust You when the journey feels overwhelming. Amen.

Action Step
Write down three areas of your life where you need to prepare—not out of fear, but out of love.

From Call to Courtroom

I became my sister's medical guardian in a hospital room filled with machines, prayers, and uncertainty. She was in a coma, and her newborn son needed care.

Because I had guardianship over her, I also became the temporary guardian of her baby. Child Protective Services (CPS) got involved due to drugs in his system at birth. My mom wanted to take him, but because of her past court case, she was denied at the last minute.

That's when the call came. My mom was panicked. I had no time to plan, no time to think—just action. I called the caseworker and told her, "I'll take him home."

That night, I completed foster care certification, background checks, emergency training, and medication handling. I left work, took the hospital classes, and went home to tell my partner, Mike. He looked at me, rolled a blunt, and said, "I guess I'll put the crib together." And just like that, we were parents again.

I became licensed not because I wanted the title, but because I needed support. Love alone doesn't pay for medical equipment or baby formula.

Two years passed. My sister struggled with addiction, missed drug tests, and couldn't complete the requirements. Eventually, her parental rights were terminated. I always said yes in court. "If rights are terminated, are you willing to adopt?" Yes. Every time. Without hesitation.

On Oakland County Adoption Day, it became official. What I always knew in my heart was written in law: he was mine.

But the journey wasn't just legal—it was emotional, spiritual, and relational. I faced rumors: She stole her sister's baby. What they didn't know was the truth: I saved him. I said yes when no one else could.

Your kids deserve a plan. Your family deserves peace. And you, Mama, deserve to be ready.

🐾 Reflection | Prayer | Affirmation | Action

From Call to Courtroom

Reflection

1. Think about the last time you had to act quickly with little preparation.
2. How did that moment reveal your resilience, faith, or resourcefulness?

Affirmation

"I am equipped with wisdom and strength for the unexpected."

Prayer

Lord, thank You for being with me in every courtroom, hospital room, and living room where decisions are made. Help me to see Your hand guiding me, even in chaos. Amen.

Action Step
Create a "Go Folder" with copies of essential documents:
- birth certificates
- medical cards
- guardianship papers
- emergency contacts

Keep it in a safe but accessible place.

My Story: Guardian, Foster Mother, and Adoptive Parent

The call came while I was at work: "Get to the hospital. Now."

But when I arrived, it wasn't a hospital room—it was a conference room. My mother was there, sobbing. Before I could even get her to speak, a team of doctors entered.

My sister was in a medically induced coma—and she was pregnant. Both she and the baby had only a slim chance of survival.

Suddenly, I was faced with life-and-death decisions: a helicopter transport, an emergency cesarean, and a hysterectomy. By God's grace, both my sister and the baby survived. But that was only the beginning.

The baby stayed in the NICU for months—his lungs underdeveloped and bruised, his tiny heart marked by holes, and his brain showing stage 3 and 4 bleeds.

My sister was also very sick. An unknown infection had ravaged her body, damaging her lungs. After the emergency delivery, doctors discovered the source: her uterus was septic and had to be removed.

Sadly, that wasn't the worst part. My sister was battling addiction. During pregnancy, she had used drugs, and after delivery, the baby tested positive. Child Protective Services (CPS) opened a case.

Because my mother was too distraught to make decisions, she called me. Guardianship passed through her to me, and suddenly I was responsible for both my sister and her newborn son.

For months, I handled everything—medical care, hospital visits, and endless decisions—while trying to hold my own life together. When CPS decided the baby would be placed in foster care, I offered to take him, but my mother wanted custody, so I stepped back.

Later, she called me crying—she'd been denied placement. I stepped in again. I called the caseworker and said, "I'll take him." She told me I'd need to complete training and sign some papers.

I trained overnight in medical care—oxygen tanks, apnea monitors, medications—and brought him home the next day.

For two years, I balanced motherhood, work, medical appointments, and the foster care process. My sister never regained custody. Her rights were terminated, and I adopted our son.

Soon after, she passed away. Gossip at her funeral broke my heart—cruel rumors that I didn't love her, that I'd stolen her baby. But what they didn't know was that I had saved them both, more than once—out of love and duty.

People often don't understand what they cannot comprehend—and that's their burden, not mine.

By the time the adoption was finalized, I was pregnant with my youngest daughter and enduring a severe sickle cell crisis from the stress. But even in grief, I knew: God had equipped me to carry both stories.

🦬 Reflection | Prayer | Affirmation | Action

My Story

Reflection

1. What part of my story resonates with your own?
2. Where do you see yourself in these pages—through grief, resilience, or unexpected love?

Affirmation

"My story matters. God can redeem even the hardest chapters of my life."

Prayer

God, thank You for turning my pain into purpose. Heal the wounds in my family line and let my legacy be one of restoration, not brokenness. Amen.

Action Step

Take ten minutes today to write down a testimony of God's faithfulness in your life.

Share it with someone who needs encouragement.

Why I'm Telling You This

I never imagined I'd be a medical proxy, guardian, foster mother, and adoptive parent all at once.

I was thrown into it—no warning, no legal preparation, no financial safety net.

And yet I did it—with God's strength, and a whole lot of paperwork.

That's why I wrote this book:

to help you plan ahead.

Because love is powerful—but preparation is protection.

Plan for the worst, and live for the best.

🕊 Reflection | Prayer | Affirmation | Action

Why I'm Telling You This

Reflection

Why is it important for you to prepare now—for your children, family, or future guardians? What fears or hopes do you feel around that?

Affirmation

"I prepare today because I love deeply. My planning creates peace for tomorrow."

Prayer

Lord, give me courage to prepare now, even in the areas I've avoided. Let my preparation be an act of love and stewardship. Cover my children and their future with Your perfect plan. Amen.

Action Step

Schedule a time this week to begin (or update) your guardianship plan, will, or power of attorney. Write one page of instructions for your children's care.

Part I: The Unexpected Call

Chapter 1: The Day Everything Changed — Becoming a Medical Guardian

I didn't plan to be anyone's legal guardian that day.

I was just a sister, standing near a cold hospital room, praying for a miracle. My sister lay in an induced coma, and her newborn—my nephew—was fighting for his life.

Machines beeped, doctors rushed in and out, and I stood there, both helpless and suddenly fully responsible.

One minute, I was working. The next, I was making medical decisions for two lives. Because I was legally named as my sister's guardian, the hospital turned to me for choices about her care—and about her newborn's future.

No one teaches you how to breathe through that kind of weight.

No one prepares you for it. But somehow, I did.

I had to.

This chapter walks through what medical guardianship means when a loved one is incapacitated.

Why having someone legally designated is critical, and how it can save you—and your family—from chaos in a crisis.

Step-by-Step Walkthrough

1. Understand the role: A medical guardian can make healthcare decisions if someone is incapacitated. This includes consenting to procedures, choosing doctors, and managing care.
2. Know the paperwork: Legal guardianship is established through court orders or hospital designations. Without it, decisions can be delayed or given to the state.
3. Document wishes: Encourage your loved ones to share medical directives and preferences. This guides your choices and reduces stress.
4. Communicate early: Discuss responsibilities with family and co-guardians to avoid conflict.

🐘 Reflection | Prayer | Affirmation | Action

Becoming a Medical Guardian

Reflection

1. What would happen if someone needed to make life-or-death decisions for me or my child today?
2. Who would step in, and would they know my wishes?

Affirmation

"I am capable of holding hard things. Even in moments of fear, I rise with grace and grit."

Prayer

God, thank You for giving me strength I didn't even know I had. Prepare my heart for both the burden and the blessing of protecting those I love. Amen.

Action

- Make a short list of people you trust to make medical decisions for your children—or for you.
- Begin drafting a medical directive or guardianship plan with them.

Chapter 2: What Happens When a Child Tests Positive at Birth

When my nephew tested positive for drugs at birth, everything shifted.

I wasn't just a family member anymore—I became his emergency advocate.

Hospitals followed protocol.

Child Protective Services (CPS) stepped in. Suddenly, there was talk of foster care, court orders, and emergency placement.

Even if you are ready to step in, without proper paperwork and planning, your love doesn't hold legal weight.

This chapter explains how CPS responds, what protocols are triggered, and what families can do to step in early

—before a child is placed with strangers.

Step-by-Step Walkthrough

1. Immediate hospital protocol: The hospital must report positive drug tests to CPS for investigation.
2. CPS assessment: CPS determines if the child can safely remain with a parent, needs temporary placement, or requires emergency foster care.
3. Family intervention: As a relative, you can request emergency kinship placement and provide evidence of your ability to care for the child.
4. Documentation: Gather identification, proof of residence, income verification, and a plan for the child's care.

🐝 Reflection | Prayer | Affirmation | Action

When a Child Tests Positive at Birth

Reflection

1. Have I considered how my family would respond to an emergency like this?
2. Am I prepared to step in if needed?

Affirmation

"Even in crisis, I can choose to show up with love, strength, and clarity."

Prayer

Lord, help me be a safe place for children in crisis. Open my eyes to the systems at work and show me how to stand in the gap. Amen.

Action

- Research your state's child protection laws and emergency kinship care process.
- Write down the hotline number or agency name in your phone or planner.

Chapter 3: Emergency Guardianship — What You Need to Know

The night I got that call, I didn't hesitate.

I left work, got certified at the hospital, and became both a guardian and foster mother within hours.

That's how emergency guardianship works when a baby's life is on the line—you act fast.

Most people don't realize that this level of caregiving requires formal steps, even when you're family.

You may need medical training, background checks, and in some cases, foster licensing.

It feels overwhelming, but it is possible—especially with guidance.

Step-by-Step Walkthrough

1. Immediate action: Respond quickly to hospital or CPS requests for placement.
2. Documentation: Complete emergency guardianship forms, background checks, and consent forms.
3. Training: Attend hospital orientation and any required caregiver training for medical or safety protocols.
4. Ongoing communication: Maintain contact with caseworkers and medical staff to stay informed and advocate effectively.

🦬 Reflection | Prayer | Affirmation | Action

Emergency Guardianship

Reflection

1. What emergency role could I imagine stepping into for someone I love?
2. How would I prepare for it now, before crisis strikes?

Affirmation

"Even when the unexpected shows up, I rise with courage and faith."

Prayer

God, thank You for guiding my steps when there's no time to think. Help me act with wisdom and compassion for every child placed in my care. Amen.

Action

- Find out who currently has legal guardianship over your children—or who you'd trust to step in.
- Write down your top two emergency guardianship choices and share your wishes with them.

Chapter 4: Love and Legalities — Why I Became a Foster Parent

People didn't always understand. Some assumed I "took" my sister's baby—as if it were a fight or betrayal.

But what they didn't see were the oxygen tanks, sleepless nights, medications, tracheostomy care, and weekly doctor visits.

What they didn't understand was love backed by legal protection.

Becoming a licensed foster parent wasn't about control. It was about access to medical resources, therapies, and case management that a relative caregiver might not otherwise receive.

Licensing gave structure and security for both my nephew, myself and our family.

Step-by-Step Walkthrough

1. Research state foster care requirements: Each state has unique licensing steps, paperwork, and training.
2. Prepare your home: Safe space, basic medical equipment, and emergency plans.
3. Training and certification: Attend required courses for safety, trauma care, and child development.
4. Ongoing case management: Stay in contact with social workers and medical providers; document all care and medical needs.

🕊 Reflection | Prayer | Affirmation | Action

Love and Legalities

Reflection

Has love ever required me to do something hard, complicated, or misunderstood by others?

Affirmation

"I honor my truth and do what's best, even when others don't understand my path."

Prayer

Lord, thank You for love that shows up in action. Strengthen me for the hard roads and protect my peace from judgment or misunderstanding. Amen.

Action

- Look into kinship foster care requirements in your county or state.
- Begin assembling necessary documents, including identification, proof of residence, and medical records.

Side Quest: Emergency Planning Toolkit for Warrior Moms

These pages are meant to give you peace of mind and prepare your family for the unexpected.

In Case of Emergency — Instructions for My Children's Care

(Place this page in a visible and accessible location — e.g., inside your emergency binder or on the fridge in a sealed envelope.)

Parent/Guardian Full Name:
_____

Date of Completion: _____

Primary Emergency Contacts:

- Name: _____ |
  Relationship: _____ |
  Phone: _____
- Name: _____ |
  Relationship: _____ |
  Phone: _____

Children's Full Names & Dates of Birth:

1. _____
2. _____
3. _____
4. _____
5.
6.

Medical Information (per child):

Allergies, medications, diagnoses, doctors, and insurance details:

Location of Important Documents:

☐ Birth Certificates

☐ Insurance Cards

☐ Medical Records

☐ Guardianship Documents

☐ School/IEP Info

☐ Other: _____

Temporary Emergency Care Instructions:

• Who has permission to pick up or temporarily care for my children:

_____

• Where the children should be taken (preferred hospital, relative, etc.):

• Important routines or care instructions (meds, oxygen, therapies, etc.):

Spiritual/Emotional Notes:

• Pastor, counselor, or church family to notify:

_____

• Words of comfort or guidance to be read to my child:

Planning Ahead — Guardianship & Legacy Checklist

Use this checklist to help create a formal guardianship and prepare your children's future if something unexpected happens.

Legal Documents

☐ Appoint a legal guardian in your will

☐ Draft a temporary guardianship letter (short-term emergency)

☐ Name a successor guardian (backup)

☐ Consult with an estate attorney or legal clinic

☐ Keep a copy with your emergency binder or planning file

Communication

☐ Talk with your chosen guardian(s) about your wishes

☐ Inform close family or friends of your plan

☐ Provide written parenting values or routines (discipline, education, faith, etc.)

☐ Share medical, school, and therapy information as needed

Financial Preparation

☐ Set up life insurance or savings to support your child's care

☐ Designate a trustee or financial guardian if needed

☐ Document passwords, account access, and debts

☐ Leave basic financial instructions for your children's guardian

Spiritual & Emotional Legacy

☐ Write a letter to your child(ren) to be read if you pass away

☐ Include Scriptures, affirmations, or family values you want passed down

☐ Create a small memory box or folder of keepsakes and photos

☐ Record a video or voice note expressing your love and legacy

Ongoing Updates

☐ Review guardianship plans yearly or after major life events

☐ Update contact information, medical details, and insurance changes regularly

☐ Revisit the plan after custody, marriage, divorce, illness, or birth of another child

Part II: Navigating Foster Care as Family

Chapter 5: The First Night Home — Baby, Equipment & Overwhelm

That first night home with my nephew is one I'll never forget.

Because of his extensive medical needs, he came with machines, medication schedules, a heart monitor, and a whole new rhythm of life.

I was scared. I was exhausted. I was still grieving my sister's condition—and now I was responsible for a medically fragile newborn.

No one handed me a manual. I had to figure it out in real time. From waking every two hours for feeding and meds to learning how to operate and change an oxygen tank. I had to become nurse, mom, and warrior all at once.

This chapter shares what it's really like to bring a medically fragile child into your home with little to no preparation.

It also includes tips to help you survive those first critical days with grace and structure.

Tips & Steps for the First Night Home:

- Set up a "command center": A bedside basket with meds, monitors, instructions, and emergency contacts.
- Create a feeding & medication schedule: Use a printed sheet or phone app to track times accurately.
- Know your equipment: Spend extra time practicing with monitors, oxygen tanks, and trach care before you leave the hospital.
- Prepare for sleep shifts: Rotate caregiving responsibilities if possible; use alarms to avoid mistakes.
- Build a support system: Have someone on-call for advice, babysitting, or even moral support.

🦋 Reflection | Prayer | Affirmation | Action

The First Night Home

Reflection
1. What fears or feelings come up when I think about sudden caregiving responsibilities?
2. How would I handle them with grace?

Affirmation
Even when I feel overwhelmed, I trust that God is equipping me moment by moment.

Prayer
Dear God, when everything feels new and heavy, be my peace. Strengthen my hands, calm my heart, and remind me I'm not in this alone. Amen

Action
Create an emergency space in your home—a basket, shelf, or drawer—for unexpected caregiving needs.

Things like:
- diapers
- wipes
- extra blanket
- phone numbers
- meds, etc.

Chapter 6: Becoming a Licensed Foster Parent (Fast!)

I didn't even have time to second-guess it.

The caseworker told me what I needed to do, to receive any help for care and I did it. Background checks. CPR training. Hospital courses on medical equipment. I became a licensed foster parent in record time—because love demanded urgency.

Many people don't know that family members can (and often should) become licensed foster parents when taking in a relative.

Not only does it give you access to resources and services, but it provides legitimacy and protection when dealing with the system.

Steps for Becoming a Licensed Foster Parent Quickly:

1. Contact your local foster care agency and explain your kinship situation.
2. Complete required training: CPR, first aid, emergency response, and specialized care for medically fragile children.
3. Submit background checks for all adults in your home.
4. Prepare your home: Safety checks, sleeping arrangements, storage for medications and equipment.
5. Document everything: Keep records of training, certifications, and hospital care instructions.
6. Work closely with caseworkers: Ask questions and request clarifications on requirements.

🕊 Reflection | Prayer | Affirmation | Action

Becoming a Licensed Foster Parent (Fast!)

Reflection

Do I know the steps to become a licensed foster parent in my state or county?

Affirmation

I am resourceful, capable, and supported—even when the process is new.

Prayer

God, lead me through unfamiliar systems with wisdom and favor. Open the right doors quickly and equip me with what I need to care well for this child. Amen

Action

Visit your state's foster care licensing website and write down the steps required for kinship caregivers.

Save it for yourself or someone else who may need it.

Chapter 7: Loving Through the System — Home Visits, Court, and Red Tape

I quickly learned that foster care is more than love.

It's paperwork, home visits, caseworker check-ins, evaluations, and court hearings. I had to keep every receipt, document every doctors/nurse visit, and meet with multiple people to prove I was capable of loving the child I was already raising with my whole heart.

There were days I wanted to scream. To walk away. But I didn't. I couldn't. Because even when the system is broken, a child's life is still shaped by what we do next.

Tips for Surviving Foster Care System Challenges:

- Create a caregiving binder or digital folder for documents, appointments, medications, and notes.
- Track everything consistently: Diapers, feeds, medication times, doctor visits.
- Communicate clearly and professionally with caseworkers, therapists, and doctors.
- Know your rights and responsibilities: Familiarize yourself with kinship foster care laws in your state.

- Build emotional support: Lean on faith communities, friends, or counseling for stress relief.
- Set boundaries: Be firm but compassionate when balancing input from multiple adults in the child's life.

🦋 Reflection | Prayer | Affirmation | Action

Loving Through the System

Reflection
1. What systems or red tape have I been afraid to engage with?
2. What's holding me back from advocating fully?

Affirmation

I can navigate hard systems without letting them harden my spirit.

Prayer

Lord, give me grace for every meeting, every form, every frustrating call. Help me see the child—not just the case—and stay grounded in love.

Action

Start a caregiving binder or digital folder for documents, appointments, and notes.

Organization = protection and peace.

Chapter 8: Supporting the Birth Parent Without Losing Yourself

I loved my sister. I still do.

But loving her and doing what was best for her child were two different lanes. Watching her struggle with addiction, denial, and grief tore me apart. But I had to stay focused on the baby in my arms. That doesn't mean I didn't hurt. It means I learned how to love her from a different space.

Supporting a birth parent during a foster care situation can be painful, confusing, and exhausting.

But it's also a spiritual assignment—one that requires boundaries, compassion, and deep honesty.

Tips for Supporting the Birth Parent:

- Establish clear boundaries: Protect your emotional health while remaining compassionate.
- Separate feelings from decisions: Love them, but prioritize the child's safety and well-being.
- Document interactions: Keep notes of conversations and agreements for legal protection.
- Set expectations: Explain your role clearly to the birth parent, even when it's hard.

- Offer resources, not control: Support their treatment plans or rehab, but don't take on responsibilities that compromise the child's care.
- Use spiritual grounding: Prayer, journaling, or mentorship can help you maintain balance.

🦬 Reflection | Prayer | Affirmation | Action

Supporting the Birth Parent

Reflection

Have I been carrying guilt or confusion about doing what's best for a child, even if it hurts someone else?

Affirmation

I can love someone and still make decisions that protect a child's future.

Prayer

God, help me love deeply without losing myself. Help me honor my sister's humanity while standing firm in truth and protection. Amen.

Action

- Write a letter (you may never send) to the birth parent.
- Say what you need to say.
- Let your heart release what it's holding.

Part III: Adoption and the Power of Yes

Chapter 9: When Parental Rights Are Terminated

The moment they said it in court, my heart dropped: "Parental rights are officially terminated."

It didn't feel like a win. It didn't feel like justice. It felt like loss. My sister lost her legal right to raise her child, and I grieved that loss deeply—even while knowing it was the right decision.

Termination of parental rights (TPR) is the legal step before adoption. It's heavy. It means there's no going back. And even if it brings safety, it can also bring sadness, confusion, and family tension.

In this chapter, I'll explain what TPR means, how the courts come to this decision, and what it looks like when you're the one saying "yes" in the aftermath.

Tips & Steps After TPR:

- Understand the legal documents: Read the court orders carefully; know what rights were terminated and what responsibilities you now carry.
- Seek counseling: Grief and guilt are natural—even when you know it's right. Professional support can help you navigate emotions.

- Communicate with your child: Age-appropriate honesty builds trust. Assure them they are loved and safe.
- Document your journey: Keep a record of decisions, court filings, and your actions as a guardian—it's both practical and therapeutic.

🦬 Reflection | Prayer | Affirmation | Action

When Parental Rights Are Terminated

Reflection

What emotions come up when I think about being responsible for a child that isn't biologically mine?

Affirmation

I was chosen for this assignment. I carry it with grace, even when it's complicated.

Prayer

Lord, when I'm caught between grief and duty, help me choose love over everything.
Let me be a safe place for the child and a vessel for Your healing.

Action

- Write down your "why"—why you're willing to say yes to hard, holy work.
- Keep this list handy to ground you when the journey feels heavy.

Chapter 10: Saying Yes in the Courtroom (and What That Means)

Every court hearing ended with the same question:

"Ms. Harris, if parental rights are terminated, are you willing and capable of adopting this child?"

Every single time, my answer was yes.

But I didn't say yes lightly. I knew what it meant—emotionally, legally, financially. I said yes because love showed up when life got hard. I said yes because family doesn't always follow biology—it follows calling.

This chapter helps you understand what it means to say yes to permanency through adoption—not just the moment in court, but the lifetime of commitment it represents.

Tips & Steps for Saying Yes to Adoption:

- Understand your responsibilities: Legal, medical, financial, and emotional duties.
- Prepare for lifelong commitment: Adoption is not just a one-time decision; it's a continuous, evolving role.
- Seek support networks: Connect with other adoptive parents or kinship caregivers.
- Plan for transition: Explain to the child that this is permanent, ensuring stability and security.

🕊 Reflection | Prayer | Affirmation | Action

Saying Yes in the Courtroom

Reflection

Where in my life have I been called to say "yes" when I didn't feel ready?

Affirmation

I do not fear commitment when love is my guide. My yes is sacred and strong.

Prayer

God, help me say yes with intention. Let my yes be a declaration of trust in You and the purpose You've placed in my life.

Action

- Research the basic steps of adoption in your state or county.
- Create a checklist of tasks to prepare legally, financially, and emotionally.

Chapter 11: Oakland County Adoption Day — Our New Beginning

Adoption Day was one of the most beautiful and emotional days of my life.

It felt like a celebration, like a baby shower for me and my son. We were surrounded by other families who had walked hard roads too.

The judge smiled, the caseworker hugged me, and the documents finally said what my heart had known all along—he was mine.

This chapter focuses less on the legal process and more on the healing that came with that moment.
There was closure.
There was joy.
There was peace.
And there was the deep, unshakable knowing that everything we had been through led us to this.

Tips for Making Adoption Day Sacred:

- Document the day: Take photos, keep programs, and write reflections.
- Celebrate intentionally: Small rituals like a special meal, prayer, or gift exchange can mark the transition.
- Involve your support system: Include mentors, family, or friends who were part of your journey.
- Reflect spiritually: Acknowledge God's presence in the triumph and hardship.

Reflection | Prayer | Affirmation | Action

Oakland County Adoption Day

Reflection

What moments in my life felt like sacred closure or new beginnings?

Affirmation

My journey may be messy, but it is meaningful. I celebrate what God has made new.

Prayer

Lord, thank You for moments that seal Your promises. Thank You for joy after long seasons of endurance. Help me celebrate fully, without guilt or hesitation.

Action

Create a small "Adoption Day" folder—photos, memories, paperwork, or letters.
Commemorate the beginning of your new chapter.

Chapter 12: Helping a Medically Fragile Child Thrive

When I first brought my son home, he was fragile.

Oxygen tanks, monitors, near-blindness, heart issues—he came with a list of diagnoses that made my head spin. But I saw something in him:

fight.

And so I fought with him.

I learned every piece of equipment, followed every therapy plan, showed up to every appointment.

We created routines. We laughed, even through tears. Over time, he didn't just survive—he thrived.

This chapter is for those raising children with special medical needs.

It includes both encouragement and practical tips that helped me go from overwhelmed to empowered.

Tips & Steps for Raising a Medically Fragile Child:

- Create a care calendar: Include meds, feeds, appointments, therapy sessions, and rest periods.
- Break tasks into routines: Consistency builds security for both child and caregiver.
- Use checklists: Medication, oxygen, monitors, and supplies. Tick off items to avoid mistakes.
- Educate yourself: Ask doctors, therapists, and nurses for hands-on demonstrations.
- Build your support team: Family, friends, home nurses, and mentors who can step in.
- Celebrate small wins: Even a milestone like a full night's sleep or a therapy breakthrough is huge.

Reflection | Prayer | Affirmation | Action

Helping a Medically Fragile Child Thrive

Reflection

What areas of my caregiving have grown because of my commitment—not my confidence?

Affirmation

I am a student and a warrior. I learn what love requires, and I rise to meet it.

Prayer

God, give me strength in the hard days, and joy in the small wins. Teach me to see progress where others see problems.

Action

Make a "care calendar" or checklist for medical or therapy needs.
Keep it simple but consistent—it becomes your lifeline.

Part IV: Family, Grief & False Narratives

Chapter 13: The Rumors Hurt, But I Know My Truth

People love a good story—even when it's not true.

I heard whispers about me—ugly ones.
"She took her sister's baby and won't give him back."
"Why is she crying now? She didn't even like her sister."

The cruelty of it hit me like a second loss, layered on top of everything I was already carrying.

But I held on to what I knew: I showed up. I stayed. I cared for both of them. I didn't "take" anyone. I saved a child. I sacrificed comfort, time, and peace to make sure my nephew had a fighting chance—and no amount of gossip will rewrite that truth.

This chapter is about standing firm in your purpose, even when others twist the narrative.

Tips & Steps for Handling Gossip and Rumors:

- Document your actions: Keep a journal of your decisions, appointments, and advocacy—proof of your integrity if needed.
- Set personal boundaries: Limit conversations with those who spread negativity. Protect your mental health.
- Seek supportive community: Lean on friends, mentors, or spiritual advisors who know your heart.
- Focus on the child: Your energy impacts the child more than anyone else's opinions.

🦋 Reflection | Prayer | Affirmation | Action

The Rumors Hurt, But I Know My Truth

Reflection

Have I ever been misunderstood or judged while doing something out of love?

Affirmation

Their opinions do not define my truth. I walk boldly in the assignment God gave me.

Prayer

God, protect my heart from the arrows of judgment. Remind me that Your approval is enough. Keep me grounded in truth, even when it's lonely.

Action

Write a letter to yourself listing the ways you've shown up with integrity.
Keep it for the days you need to remember who you are.

Chapter 14: Loving My Sister While Telling the Truth

I loved my sister. Still do.

But love isn't the same as denial. She made choices—some heartbreaking ones. And I carried the weight of her consequences.

For a long time, I felt torn: honor her memory or be honest about what happened? But the truth is, both can exist.

I can love her and still name the pain. I can remember her beauty while acknowledging her battles.

She wasn't perfect—but she was still mine.

This chapter is about honoring complicated relationships and choosing truth as an act of love—not betrayal.

Tips & Steps for Speaking Truth in Love:

- Use "I" statements: Speak from your experience to avoid blame.
- Set boundaries: Decide which conversations are healthy and which are toxic.
- Document memories: Journaling or letters can help process complex feelings.
- Teach by example: Model honesty, integrity, and compassion for children and family.

🦋 Reflection | Prayer | Affirmation | Action

Loving My Sister While Telling the Truth

Reflection

What relationships in my life have layers of both love and pain?

Affirmation

I can speak truth and still walk in love. Honesty is not disrespect—it is healing.

Prayer

Lord, help me tell the whole story—love, pain, failure, and redemption. Let my honesty be healing for others and peace for my soul. Amen

Action
Write down one thing you miss about your loved one and one truth you need to release about them.

Let both exist together.

Chapter 15: The Grief No One Prepared Me For

There is a grief that comes when someone dies. And there is another grief when they are still alive but can no longer be who they were.

I grieved my sister long before she passed. I grieved the way addiction changed her. I grieved the parts of our relationship that never healed. And, when she died, I had to grieve her all over again.

And I had to do all that while raising our son.

This chapter is about the hidden grief—the kind people don't talk about, the kind you carry in silence while still trying to function.

If you've ever had to keep going through heartbreak, this one's for you.

Tips & Steps for Processing Hidden Grief:
- Name your grief: Write down emotions and memories to validate your experience.
- Set aside quiet time: Even 10–15 minutes of intentional reflection daily helps.
- Seek spiritual guidance: Prayer, meditation, or scripture can bring perspective.
- Engage supportive people: Therapists, mentors, or support groups provide safe spaces to process.
- Create rituals: Candles, memory boxes, or letters can honor loss tangibly.

🕊 Reflection | Prayer | Affirmation | Action

The Grief No One Prepared Me For

Reflection

Where am I still grieving something—or someone—I never had the space to fully mourn?

Affirmation

I give myself permission to grieve fully and freely. My tears are not weakness; they are worship.

Prayer

God, hold me in the parts of my story that still ache. Let my grief bring me closer to Your comfort and not farther from myself. Amen

Action

Light a candle, take a quiet walk, or say their name out loud.

Honor your grief in a tangible way today.

Chapter 16: When Family Feels Divided — Speaking Up With Grace

Family pain hits different.

Especially when the same people who should support you become the ones whispering behind your back.

After my sister passed, it felt like the judgment and distance got worse—not better.

I had to learn how to protect my peace while still showing up in love. I had to set boundaries. I had to correct lies without fueling more fire. And I had to accept that some relationships would never be what they were.

This chapter helps you navigate family tension with grace and truth—and teaches how to hold your peace without forfeiting your voice.

Tips & Steps for Navigating Family Conflict:

- Identify your non-negotiables: Decide what you will and won't tolerate.
- Use calm communication: Avoid raising your voice; stick to facts and "I" statements.
- Accept limitations: Some family members may never understand. Release expectations.
- Prioritize the child: Keep focus on what's best for the child, not pleasing everyone.
- Create safe spaces: Journals, prayer, or a trusted friend can help you vent without escalation.

🕊 Reflection | Prayer | Affirmation | Action

When Family Feels Divided

Reflection

What boundaries do I need to protect my peace within my family?

Affirmation

I can speak truthfully and lovingly. I choose grace without sacrificing clarity.

Prayer

Lord, help me navigate family dynamics with wisdom. Let my words bring light, not fire. Give me the courage to stand in truth and the humility to release what I cannot control. Amen

Action

- Write out 1–2 clear boundary statements you can use when conversations become harmful or triggering.
- Practice them in a calm tone. Role-play if needed to build confidence.

Part V: Planning for the Unplanned

Chapter 17: How to Legally Name a Guardian for Your Child

You never think you'll have to plan for someone else raising your child. But life has a way of teaching us:

hope is not a strategy.

And love—real love—plans ahead.

Watching what happened with my sister's medical collapse, then her rights being terminated, reminded me how important it is to have legal guardianship paperwork in place before crisis hits.

If something were to happen to me, I couldn't bear the thought of my children entering the system because I didn't take the time to prepare.

This chapter walks you through how to legally name a guardian, even if you don't have a lawyer.

This is not just paperwork—it's peace of mind.

Tips & Steps for Naming a Legal Guardian:

- Choose carefully: Pick someone who shares your values, parenting style, and vision for the child's life.
- Have a conversation first: Make sure they are willing and understand the responsibilities.
- Use official forms: Each state has its own legal guardianship forms—download from your state government website.
- Include alternates: Life is unpredictable; name a backup guardian.
- Review regularly: Life changes, so review and update every few years or after major life events.
- Keep documents accessible: Store copies with your attorney, in a safe at home, or digitally with trusted access.

🕊 Reflection | Prayer | Affirmation | Action

How to Legally Name a Guardian for Your Child

Reflection

Have I named someone I trust to care for my children if I'm no longer able?

Affirmation

Because I love my children, I plan for their future—even when it's hard.

Prayer

Lord, guide me in choosing the right person to care for my children if I can't. Give me peace in my decisions and courage to follow through.

Action

- Download or request your state's guardianship form.
- Write down your top two choices and have a conversation with them this week.

Chapter 18: How to Become a Foster Parent in Your State

I didn't plan to become a foster parent—it happened out of necessity, love, and urgency.

But once I said yes, I realized how much I didn't know. Thankfully, I found support systems, agencies, and mentors to guide me through the process.

I was blessed to have a caseworker Ms.E that literally held my hand through it all. During her visits I would ask all kinds of questions, and she helped me get the answers and support we needed.

If you're considering becoming a licensed foster parent—especially to care for kin or medically fragile children—this chapter will help you understand what to expect.

Every state is different, but the core steps are similar: application, training, background checks, home study, and ongoing support.

You don't need to be perfect. You just need to be willing—and prepared.

Tips & Steps to Becoming a Foster Parent:

- Research your state: Each state has unique requirements and paperwork.
- Prepare your home: Safe sleeping arrangements, child-proofing, and emergency contacts.
- Training is key: Most states require CPR, first aid, and foster care orientation.
- Expect a home study: A social worker evaluates your home environment, lifestyle, and readiness.
- Gather documentation: ID, background checks, medical records, references, and proof of income.
- Mentorship: Connect with experienced foster parents to guide you through challenges.

🦬 Reflection | Prayer | Affirmation | Action

How to Become a Foster Parent in Your State

Reflection

What fears or beliefs have stopped me from exploring foster care before?

Affirmation

I am capable of learning, growing, and becoming the safe place a child needs.

Prayer

God, if this path is for me, show me the way. Provide the resources, strength, and support I need to take the first step. Amen

Action

- Search online: "How to become a foster parent in [your state]."
- Bookmark the official government or foster care agency website and explore their requirements.

Chapter 19: Kinship & Family Adoption — What You Need to Know

When you adopt a child within your family, the process can be both comforting and confusing.

Comforting—because the child is already connected to you. Confusing—because the legal process doesn't feel any simpler just because you share DNA.

In my case, kinship foster care led to legal adoption. But there were still hoops, evaluations, background checks, and court hearings.

This chapter walks you through what to expect during a kinship adoption process—including the emotional side: the fear of bureaucracy, the weight of permanence, and the deep responsibility of stepping in for family.

Tips & Steps for Kinship Adoption:

- Ask for guidance early: Talk to local agencies, social workers, or an attorney specializing in adoption.
- Document your caregiving: Logs, photos, and notes can help courts see your commitment.
- Stay patient: Legal processes take time, even for family.
- Prepare emotionally: Adoption solidifies the legal parent-child relationship, but emotional bonds are ongoing work.
- Financial planning: Understand costs, possible subsidies, or support for kinship families.

🕊 Reflection | Prayer | Affirmation | Action

Kinship & Family Adoption

Reflection

What fears or myths have I believed about adopting a family member?

Affirmation

I am not just stepping in—I am stepping up. My love and commitment are enough.

Prayer

Lord, give me wisdom and strength to walk through kinship adoption with patience, grace, and the best interest of the child in mind. Amen

Action

- Write down 3 questions you have about kinship adoption.
- Take the first step by contacting a local agency or attorney for answers.

Chapter 20: Getting Your House, Heart & Finances Ready for a Child

Let me be honest: I was not "ready."

I didn't have a fancy nursery or perfect budget. I had faith, a safe space, and an overwhelming amount of love. And that was a powerful start.

Still, when a child enters your home—especially in crisis—it affects every part of your life: your sleep, your schedule, your finances, and your heart.

This chapter helps you prepare practically and emotionally. We'll cover home prep, medical equipment (if applicable), budgeting, and the emotional toll no one talks about.

Tips & Steps for Preparation:

- Home: Safety-proof your home, create a sleep and play area, and gather essentials.
- Finances: Track monthly expenses, consider emergency funds, and explore support programs or subsidies.
- Medical: If caring for a medically fragile child, learn about equipment, medications, and appointment scheduling.

- Emotional: Create a support network and establish personal self-care routines.
- Flexibility: Accept that "ready" is relative—presence, love, and structure matter more than perfection.

Reflection | Prayer | Affirmation | Action

Getting Your House, Heart & Finances Ready

Reflection

What does "ready" really mean for me—and what can I start preparing today?

Affirmation

I don't have to be perfect. I only have to be present, prayerful, and prepared in the ways I can.

Prayer

Father, give me peace in the unknown and strength for the days ahead. Remind me that You equip those You call.

Action
Make a checklist:
- One small home task (organize baby's room, set up a safe space)
- One financial task (track expenses, set up budget)
- One heart-centered self-care task (prayer, meditation, journaling)
  Complete at least one this week to start preparing.

Part VI: The Legacy of Preparation

Chapter 21: Why Every Parent Needs a Guardian Plan

I never imagined I'd be in court fighting for guardianship over my sister's child. But I also never imagined that a medical emergency could shift a family's structure overnight.

The truth is, many of us avoid thinking about what will happen to our children if we become unable to care for them.
It's uncomfortable, and we tell ourselves we'll handle it "later." But the most loving thing we can do is prepare now.

In this chapter, I'll walk you through what a guardian plan is, why it's essential, and how it can protect your children from uncertainty and the foster care system—even if you're not "wealthy" or "ready."

You don't need to have everything together.

You just need to have a plan.

Tips & Steps for a Guardian Plan:

- Identify trusted individuals: Choose two people who share your values and parenting style.
- Document your wishes: Write down what matters most for your child's upbringing, education, and healthcare.
- Legal paperwork: Consider a guardian designation form or a legal letter. Consult an attorney if possible.
- Communicate openly: Talk to your chosen guardians so they understand your expectations.
- Review and update: Life changes; revisit your plan every 1–2 years or after major life events.

Reflection | Prayer | Affirmation | Action

Why Every Parent Needs a Guardian Plan

Reflection

What's stopping me from making a guardian plan—and what could happen if I don't?

Affirmation

Because I love my child, I prepare today—not just for myself, but for their future.

Prayer

Lord, give me the wisdom to plan well and the peace to know that preparation is not fear—it's faith in action. Amen

Action

- Write down the names of two trusted people you would consider as guardians.
- Begin drafting a simple guardian letter or contact an attorney for next steps.

Chapter 22: Leaving Instructions — Wills, Letters & Life Insurance

It's not just about what you leave behind—it's about what you leave in place.

One of the most powerful gifts you can leave your children is clarity: a clear will, a letter of love and instruction, a life insurance policy—even a small one—that helps cover their care.

Too often, families fall into confusion and conflict after loss simply because nothing was written down.

This chapter isn't about fear—it's about stewardship.

I'll break down how to write a simple will, what to include in a guardian letter, and how to find affordable life insurance as a single mom or someone with a chronic illness.

It's not about being rich—it's about being responsible.

Tips & Steps for Leaving Instructions:

- Simple will: Outline guardianship, asset distribution, and any other important wishes.
- Guardian letter: Include child care preferences, routines, values, and emergency contacts.
- Life insurance: Even a modest policy can help cover living expenses, education, or special needs.
- Organize your documents: Keep copies with a trusted family member, attorney, or digital secure folder.
- Communicate: Let your child's guardian and key family members know where your documents are stored.

Reflection | Prayer | Affirmation | Action

Leaving Instructions

Reflection

What would I want my children (or loved ones) to know if I were gone tomorrow?

Affirmation

I choose to lead with love by planning in peace. My words, written today, will guide hearts tomorrow.

Prayer

God, help me write the words I've avoided. Let my planning reflect my love. Give me wisdom as I put instructions in place.

Action

1. Start your "legacy binder."
2. Write a draft of a personal letter to your child.
3. Include emergency contacts, insurance info, and any existing legal documents.

Chapter 22 (Part 2): Legacy Planning – My Instructions of Love

1. My Guardian Choices

Who would I trust to care for my child(ren) if something happened to me?

- First Choice:
  _____
  Phone/Contact:
  _____
  Reason:
  _____

- Second Choice (Backup):
  _____
  Phone/Contact:
  _____
  Reason:
  _____

2. My Will & Legal Docs

☐ I have a simple will
☐ I've written a guardian letter
☐ I've shared my wishes with trusted family/friends
☐ I have life insurance (even a small policy)

3. Personal Letter to My Child(ren)

Start a draft of your letter here. Let your words be filled with peace, love, and legacy.

Dear [Child's Name],
I want you to always remember...

Reflection Prompt:
What's one step I will take this week to prepare my guardian or legacy plan?

Chapter 23: Creating a Legacy of Love (and Legal Readiness)

Legacy isn't just about money—it's about meaning.

When I think about legacy now, I think about the child I adopted, the sister I loved through crisis, the nights I stayed up rocking a medically fragile baby, and the paperwork I filled out with trembling hands.

All of it—every piece—was legacy-building.

Your legacy is in how you love. And how you prepare that love to outlast you.

This chapter will guide you through creating a legacy on paper, in memory, and through intention.

Whether you have a trust fund or just a trunk of memories, this is your reminder that you are the legacy.

Tips & Steps for Legacy Planning:

- Collect memories: Photos, letters, journals, and milestones.
- Document lessons: Write life lessons, faith principles, and family values.
- Organize legal documents: Keep wills, guardianship papers, and insurance info accessible.
- Create a story: A personal letter or memory book for your child(ren).
- Begin now: Legacy isn't about waiting—it's about daily choices and intentional documentation.

🕊 Reflection | Prayer | Affirmation | Action

Creating a Legacy of Love

Reflection

What do I want to be remembered for—and how can I begin living that legacy now?

Affirmation

My life is a legacy in motion. Every act of preparation is an act of love.

Prayer

Lord, Thank You for entrusting me with this life, this love, this family. Help me live and leave a legacy of faith, courage, and clarity. Amen

Action

- Make a "legacy list"—five things (letters, photos, documents, lessons) you want to leave for your children or loved ones.
- Start collecting or creating them this month.

Chapter 24: Helping Other Moms Do the Same

Once you've lived through it, you carry a sacred kind of wisdom.

There's another mom out there right now—exhausted, scared, unprepared—facing the same crisis you once did. She needs what you now know. And you don't need a platform to help her. You just need to show up.

This chapter encourages you to share your knowledge. Whether it's helping a friend set up guardianship paperwork, donating a car seat, or telling your story—your voice matters. You're not just a survivor.

You're a mentor, a light, and a way-maker for the next woman behind you.

Tips & Steps for Helping Others:
- Mentor informally: Even a quick conversation or checklist can change a mom's path.
- Share resources: Guardianship forms, foster care guides, or parenting tips.
- Lead with empathy: Everyone's journey is different—listen first, guide second.
- Encourage planning: Emphasize preparation as an act of love, not fear.

🦋 Reflection | Prayer | Affirmation | Action

Helping Other Moms Do the Same

Reflection

How can I use my story to help someone else prepare?

Affirmation

What I've lived through is someone else's survival guide. My voice is needed.

Prayer

God, show me who I can help. Give me the courage to speak, the wisdom to serve, and the grace to walk with others through what I've overcome. Amen

Action

- Reach out to one mom this week.
- Share a resource, a checklist, or just encouragement.
  Your story might be the thing that changes hers.

Letter from the Author

Mama,

If you've made it to the end of this book, I want you to know something sacred: You are not alone.

What you're carrying is heavy. Parenting through crisis, illness, poverty, and grief is something no guidebook truly prepares you for. But you're doing it. Even when your knees shake. Even when the family whispers. Even when the court doesn't see your tears.

I wrote this book because I've been there. Because I am there. I wrote it for the version of me who needed someone to say,
"You're not crazy. You're not selfish. You're just overwhelmed—and doing the best you can."

So wherever you are in this journey—becoming a guardian, fighting for a child, preparing your own legacy—I want to say:
You are brave. You are called. And you are chosen for this.

And if no one has told you today—I'm proud of you. Stay the course. The world needs more warrior moms like you.

With deep love, Shaun

Scriptures for Love, Courage & Trust

1 Corinthians 13:4-7 (NLT)

Love is patient and kind. It is not jealous or boastful... Love never gives up.

Joshua 1:9 (NIV)

Be strong and courageous. Do not be afraid; do not be discouraged, for the Lord your God will be with you wherever you go.

Romans 12:10 (NLT)

Be devoted to one another in love. Honor one another above yourselves.

1 John 4:18 (NLT)

There is no fear in love. But perfect love drives out fear.

Closing Prayer:

Lord, teach me to love boldly, to trust You completely, and to walk in courage even when it feels uncomfortable.

Book Club / Group Discussion Questions

Use these questions in your book club, women's group, or support circle.

Part I: The Unexpected Call

1. How did you feel reading Shaundra's emergency call experience? Have you ever faced a life-altering decision in a moment's notice?
2. What do you believe helped her say yes to guardianship?

Part II: Foster Care as Family

3. What are the emotional and spiritual costs of stepping into foster care for a relative?
4. How can we better support kinship caregivers in our communities?

Part III: Adoption & Advocacy

5. What did "saying yes in the courtroom" represent for the author?
6. How can we celebrate and support adoptive moms—especially those stepping in from within the family?

Part IV: Grief & Grace

7. What did this book teach you about grief and complicated family dynamics?
8. Have you ever had to speak your truth at the risk of being misunderstood?

Part V & VI: Legacy Planning

9. What surprised you about the guardianship, will, or life insurance processes?
10. What steps are you now inspired to take to create a plan for your children?

For Reflection & Continued Growth

Journaling Prompt:

> How is God inviting me to love beyond fear in this season?
>
> What does "family" mean to me when I let go of control and lean into faith?

Recommended Next Read:

> The Warrior Mom's Guide to Legacy: Building Faith, Family, and Futures That Last.

Glossary of Key Terms

Adoption

A legal process that permanently transfers all parental rights and responsibilities from a child's birth parents to another individual or couple. Adoption provides a forever home and full legal recognition as a parent.

Advocate

A person who speaks or acts on behalf of someone else. In this book, it often refers to a caregiver standing up for a child's needs in medical, legal, or school systems.

Case Plan

A written document created by Child Protective Services (CPS) outlining goals, services, and timelines for both the child and the family. It helps guide decisions about reunification or adoption.

Caseworker / Social Worker

A professional responsible for managing a child's placement, supporting the caregiver, and ensuring the child's safety and well-being throughout the foster or guardianship process.

CPS (Child Protective Services)

A government agency that investigates reports of child abuse or neglect and determines whether intervention or placement is needed to protect the child.

Emergency Guardianship

A temporary legal arrangement allowing an approved adult to make immediate decisions for a child or incapacitated person when no parent or guardian is available.

Foster Care

A temporary living situation for children who cannot safely remain with their biological parents. Foster care can involve relatives (kinship care) or licensed foster parents.

Guardian / Legal Guardian

An individual appointed by a court to care for and make decisions for a minor or incapacitated adult. Guardianship can be temporary, permanent, or limited to specific decisions (such as medical care).

Guardianship Agreement

A legal document that names who will care for a child if the parent is unable to do so. It may include medical, financial, and educational authority.

Home Study

An evaluation process conducted by a licensed agency or social worker to assess a prospective guardian or foster parent's readiness, home safety, and family environment.

Kinship Care

When a child is placed in the care of a relative or close family friend rather than a traditional foster home. Kinship caregivers may or may not be licensed foster parents.

Licensing (Foster Care Licensing)

The process by which caregivers become approved to provide foster care. It includes training, background checks, and a home inspection.

Medical Guardian

A person legally authorized to make healthcare decisions on behalf of another individual who is unable to make those decisions themselves.

Parental Rights

The legal rights and responsibilities a parent has toward their child, including decisions about care, education, and medical treatment. Parental rights can be temporarily suspended or permanently terminated in certain cases.

Placement

The act of placing a child into a home for temporary or long-term care. Placement decisions are made by CPS or the court system.

Power of Attorney (POA)

A legal document allowing someone to make decisions on another's behalf in specific areas such as medical or financial matters.

Reunification

The process of returning a child to their biological parent(s) after a period of foster or kinship care once safety and stability are reestablished.

Safety Plan

A written agreement developed by CPS or a caseworker to outline steps that must be taken to ensure a child's safety while remaining in or returning to a home.

Termination of Parental Rights (TPR)

A legal ruling that permanently ends the parent-child relationship, freeing the child for adoption.

Trauma-Informed Care

An approach to caregiving that recognizes the impact of trauma on a child's behavior and emotional needs and seeks to create safety, trust, and healing through compassion and consistency.

Visitation

Court-approved time for biological parents or family members to spend with a child who is in foster or kinship care, often supervised to ensure safety.

Faith & Wellness Terms

Grace – The unearned love and strength that God provides, even in seasons of weakness or uncertainty.

Resilience – The ability to recover and rise again after hardship; a spiritual and emotional muscle built through faith.

Calling – A divine invitation to act with purpose, even when it leads into unexpected places.

Legacy – The love, lessons, and faith we leave behind for the next generation.

Resources & Recommended Reading

Faith & Encouragement

- The Bible — Start with Psalm 68:6 ("God sets the lonely in families") and Isaiah 61:3 ("Beauty for ashes").
- Priscilla Shirer, Fervent: A Woman's Battle Plan for Serious, Specific, and Strategic Prayer — A powerful guide to praying with focus and authority.
- Sarah Mae & Sally Clarkson, Desperate: Hope for the Mom Who Needs to Breathe — A heartfelt reminder that you're never alone in motherhood.
- Christine Caine, Unexpected: Leave Fear Behind, Move Forward in Faith, Embrace the Adventure — Encouragement for walking in faith through life's surprises.

Legal & Guardianship Resources

(Always verify based on your state's laws or consult a family law attorney for current guidance.)

- Child Welfare Information Gateway – www.childwelfare.gov

Offers free resources on guardianship, kinship care, and adoption by state.

- American Bar Association (ABA) – Legal Guide for Guardianship – www.americanbar.org

    Explains your rights and responsibilities as a legal guardian or foster caregiver.

- National Guardianship Association – www.guardianship.org

    Provides ethical standards and educational materials for family guardians.

Foster & Adoption Support

- AdoptUSKids – www.adoptuskids.org

    Learn about foster-to-adopt programs and connect with support groups nationwide.

- The Dave Thomas Foundation for Adoption – www.davethomasfoundation.org

    Offers tools and resources to help children in foster care find forever families.

- Kinship Care Resource Center – www.kinshipcare.org

Practical and emotional support for relatives caring for children.

- Casey Family Programs – www.casey.org

Promotes safe, supportive foster systems and long-term family success.

Chronic Illness, Advocacy & Self-Care for Moms

- The Warrior Mom's Guide to GhettoOCD™ (by Shaundra M. G. Harris) — A compassionate guide to creating peace, healing, and order even in chaos.
- Rest: Why You Get More Done When You Work Less, by Alex Soojung-Kim Pang — Explores the balance of productivity and restoration.
- Boundaries, by Dr. Henry Cloud & Dr. John Townsend — Learn how to set emotional and relational boundaries without guilt.
- Chronic Joy Ministry – www.chronic-joy.org

Encouragement and faith resources for those living with chronic illness.

Practical Tools & Planning

- My Family Emergency Plan Worksheet (Downloadable template) — Create a plan for guardianship, medical decisions, and family support in emergencies.
- LegalZoom & Rocket Lawyer — Affordable online templates for medical or temporary guardianship forms.
- Power of Attorney (POA) Templates — Many state websites offer free, fillable forms. Search "[Your State] Power of Attorney Form."
- Faith-Based Foster Parent Training Programs — Ask your church or local community center about certified foster care courses that include spiritual support.

The Warrior Mom's Guide™ Book Series

FOUNDATION: The Pilot Book

♡ **A Warrior Within, A Chronic Illness**

The Warrior Mom's Guide to Sickle Cell & Chronic Resilience

My story of battling sickle cell while raising a family—woven with practical mindset shifts, survival tools, and advocacy.

📖 The heart of the Warrior Mom movement and the introduction to the series.

THE DEEP-DIVE SERIES (Books 1–10)

♡ **The Warrior Mom's Guide to GhettoOCD™** (Home Organization & Cleaning)

Practical, real-life homemaking strategies for moms with chronic illness.

✻ **The Warrior Mom's Guide to Mental Wellness & Finding Joy in the Chaos**

Therapy, prayer, and emotional survival tools for weary moms.

🤍 The Warrior Mom's Guide to Single Motherhood by Choice

Reclaiming peace, health, and wholeness after carrying it all.

🤍 The Warrior Mom's Guide to Loving Unexpectedly

Guardianship, Fostering & Adoption with Faith and Fierce Love

Finding your voice, courage, and confidence in nontraditional motherhood.

🤍 The Warrior Mom's Guide to Generational Wealth & Family Legacy

Building wealth, purpose, and a future that lasts.

🤍 The Warrior Mom's Guide to Spiritual Reset & Chronic Faith

Faith after diagnosis, grace during flare-ups, and spiritual renewal when you feel forgotten.

⚫ The Warrior Mom's Guide to ZBB & Cash Stuffing

Zero-based budgeting & cash envelope systems for sick-day survival.

🥾 The Warrior Mom's Guide to Homeschooling for the Homegirls

Practical tools for rest, rejuvenation, and chronic-illness-friendly homeschooling.

🖤 The Warrior Mom's Guide to Homeownership & Stability

Creative paths to securing a home with chronic illness and limited income.

🌿 The Warrior Mom's Guide to Living in Peace

End-of-life planning with grace: wills, medical directives, legacy projects, and restoration.

Find the books, companion workbooks, journals, planners, and more at:

www.warriormomacademy.com

About the Author

Shaundra is a devoted mother, fierce advocate, and compassionate warrior who knows firsthand the complexities of parenting through crisis.

As a licensed foster parent and adoptive mom, Shaundra's journey through medical guardianship, foster care, and adoption has inspired her to write and empower other women facing similar challenges.

Her honest storytelling, faith-driven resilience, and practical guidance help single moms—especially those navigating chronic illness and unexpected family transitions—find strength, peace, and hope.

Shaundra lives happily with her son and daughters and is passionate about community, healing, and legacy building.

Final Blessing

For the mom who never asked for the storm, but still became the shelter.

May God cover your home with peace, protection, and purpose.

May your children always feel the safety of your love, even when you're not in the room.

May your faith rise higher than fear, and your heart rest in knowing—you have done enough.

You are seen.

You are chosen.

You are equipped.

You are a Warrior Mom.

Amen.

www.ingramcontent.com/pod-product-compliance
Lightning Source LLC
Chambersburg PA
CBHW030222170426
43194CB00007BA/825